LIVING LENT

Meditations for These Forty Days

BARBARA CAWTHORNE CRAFTON

MOREHOUSE PUBLISHING

Morehouse Publishing
P.O. Box 1321
Harrisburg, PA 17105

Morehouse Publishing is a division of the Morehouse Group.

Printed in the United States of America

Cover art: *The Green Christ,* by Paul Gauguin (School of Pont-Aven), Royal Museum of Fine Arts, Brussels, Belgium

Cover design by Rick Snizik

Crafton, Barbara Cawthorne.
     Living Lent : meditations for these forty days / Barbara Cawthorne Crafton.
        p. cm.
     Includes bibliographical references.
     ISBN 0–8192–1756–5 (pbk.)
     1. Lent—Meditations. 2. Hymns—Devotional use. 3. Episcopal Church—Prayer-books and devotions—English. I. Title.
BV85.C67   1998
242'.34—dc21

98–45774
CIP

01 02 03 04 05   10 9 8 7 6 5 4 3

For my second mother,
Laura Loeffler Cawthorne.
A Lutheran.

To the Reader

Ah, Episcopal hymnody! I love the *Hymnal 1982*. I loved dear old 1940, too, with all his frumpy charms, and I greet with interest all the little nieces and nephews who've come along in recent years. I hope you sing the hymns that sparked these little meditations to yourself as your day unfolds. We're lucky to have such lovely music and poetry so near at hand. God has been very good to us.

So has Church Publishing, which has graciously allowed the use of hymn texts in this book. And the several fine publications in which a few of these meditations first appeared: *Episcopal Life, The Living Pulpit, The Journal of Women's Ministries* and the *General Theological Seminary Alumni News*. I thank them all.

Claim some minutes for quiet reflection every day. Just do it. You need and deserve it, and it's a cinch nobody else is going to do it for you. So enjoy this little book. We're allowed to enjoy things in Lent now, as long as we don't make too much noise.

BCC
New York City, 1998

Ash Wednesday

So daily dying to the way of self, so daily living to your way of love...
HYMN 149, THOMAS H. CAIN (B. 1931)

We didn't even know what moderation was. What it felt like. We didn't just work: We inhaled our jobs, sucked them in, *became* them. Stayed late, brought work home—it was never enough, though, no matter how much time we put in.

We didn't just smoke: We lit up a cigarette, only to realize that we already had one going in the ashtray.

We ordered things we didn't need from the shiny catalogs that came to our houses: We ordered three times as much as we could use, and then we ordered three times as much as our children could use.

We didn't just eat: We stuffed ourselves. We had gained only three pounds since the previous year, we told ourselves. Three pounds is not a lot. We had gained about that much in each of the twenty-five years since high school. We did not do the math.

We redid living rooms in which the furniture was not worn out. We threw away clothing that was merely out of style. We drank wine when the label on our prescriptions said it was dangerous to use alcohol while taking this medication. "They always put that on the label," we told our children when they asked about this. We saw that they were worried. We knew it was because they loved us and needed us. How innocent they were. We hastened to reassure them: "It doesn't really hurt if you're careful."

We felt that it was important to be good to ourselves, and that this meant that it was dangerous to tell ourselves no. About anything, ever. Repression of one's desires was an unhealthy thing. *I work hard*, we told ourselves. *I deserve a little treat.* We treated ourselves every day.

And if it was dangerous for us to want and not have, it was even more so for our children. They must never know what it is to want something and not have it immediately. It will make them bitter, we told ourselves. So we anticipated their needs and desires. We got them both the doll *and* the bike. If their grades were good, we got them their own telephones.

There were times, coming into the house from work or waking early when all was quiet, when we felt uneasy about the sense of entitlement that characterized all our days. When we wondered if the mad slalom between fevered overwork and excess of appetite were not two sides of the same coin. *Probably yes,* we decided at these times. Suddenly we saw it all clearly: *I am driven by my creatures— my schedule, my work, my possessions, my hungers. I do not drive them; they drive me. Probably yes. Certainly yes. This is how it is.* We arose and did twenty sit-ups. The next day the moment had passed; we did none.

After moments like that, we were awash in self-contempt. *You are weak. Self-indulgent. You are spineless about work and about everything else. You set no limits. You will become ineffective.* We bridled at that last bit, drew ourselves up to our full heights, insisted defensively on our competence, on the respect we were due because of all our hard work. We looked for others whose lives were similarly overstuffed; we found them. "This is just the way it is," we said to one another on the train, in the restaurant. "This is modern life. Maybe some people have time to measure things out by teaspoonfuls." Our voices dripped contempt for those people who had such time. We felt oddly defensive, though no one had accused us of anything. *But not me. Not anyone who has a life. I have a life. I work hard. I play hard.*

When did the collision between our appetites and the needs of our souls happen? Was there a heart attack? Did we get laid off from work, one of the thousands certified as extraneous? Did a beloved child become a bored stranger, a marriage fall silent and cold? Or, by some exquisite working of God's grace, did we just find the courage to look the truth in the eye and, for once, not blink? How did we come to know that we were dying a slow and unacknowledged death? And that the only way back to life was to set all our packages down and begin again, carrying with us only what we really needed?

We travail. We are heavy laden. Refresh us, O homeless, jobless, possession-less Savior. You came naked, and naked you go. And so it is for us. So it is for all of us.

Thursday after Ash Wednesday

Wilt thou forgive that sin, where I begun,
Which is my sin, though it were done before?
HYMN 140, JOHN DONNE (1573–1631)

The great poet is talking about original sin here, of course: The doctrine holds that we all arrive in this world already in a state of sin inherited from our first parents. Sinners without lifting a finger, all of us. This idea rubs a lot of people the wrong way: You look down at your sweet baby sighing softly in her sleep, and she just doesn't seem sinful. This tiny, perfect thing is in a state of sin? You just don't buy it.

Adam and Eve and their apple, or mango, or whatever it was that grew on that tree in the middle of the garden—is all that only about how evil got loose on the earth? This ancient story explains the fact that life is hard in terms of a primordial infringement and its permanent punishment. Most of us do the same thing. "What did I do to deserve this?" a woman asks me in the hospital, forgetting for a moment that pain and sorrow come to everyone, and that they usually have little or nothing to do with what we may or may not have done. It seems to us that there ought to be a reason for our sorrows, something we have done that we can arrange not to do anymore and thereby escape further suffering. But no. The story of Adam and Eve doesn't help us much there.

"Sin" is a hard word in this context. Original sin doesn't mean that we all come into the world with a criminal record. All it means is that we start out utterly self-absorbed, and that we're likely to stay that way unless something happens to civilize us. Now that's something we *can* affirm: Little children are self-centered, completely so. Some people stay that way their whole lives long, but most of us don't. We learn empathy as we grow.

But we learn it gradually. Setting our desires aside for the sake of a greater good doesn't come naturally to us. We must *learn* how, learn to long for greater goods than those immediately applicable to our own pleasures. Some people have learned this longing so well that they have given up their lives for others. Some have gone to their deaths with hymns of praise on their lips. What we remember daily of our first parents is not really about snakes and difficult childbirths—what we carry of them in us is our tendency to put ourselves and our desires in God's place. We recognize their sin in our hearts, and we struggle a lifetime to tame it. I may think I've made some real progress in dying to my own selfishness. Then I am shocked at how quickly it bursts into flame again, given the right set of circumstances. Me and everybody else, it appears: The apple doesn't fall very far from the tree.

Friday after Ash Wednesday

Lord Jesus, Sun of Righteousness, shine in our hearts, we pray;
dispel the gloom that shades our minds and be to us as day.
HYMN 144, LATIN TRANSLATED BY ANNE K. LECROY (B. 1930)

I remember hearing my father talk of what the Sabbath meant when he was a boy. I remember contrasting it with our own easy Sundays and feeling a little inferior: We had grown soft. They must have been better than we were—they were so grim.

Something in us wants things to be harder sometimes. Something in us wants to push ourselves, to feel what it is to be denied. Sometimes. And so, Fridays in Lent: Some people who don't even think of fasting on Fridays during the rest of the year pick it up again during these forty days. They remember the rigidities of the church of their youth—or maybe of someone else's—and feel drawn to them.

Fasting is hard—it needs to be hard, a denial of something whose absence you will notice. I am struck by my sophistry in the early days of a fast: the interior arguments I mount as to why it really would not be such a terrible thing to have a piece of pie. Didn't God make pie—or at least give humankind the wit to invent it?

It's not the piece of pie that matters. What matters is noticing its absence. It's being caught up short in the normal run of the day and remembering something that is not normal: The love of God is not normal, not human, not ordinary. It is self-giving, self-sacrificial. By doing something out of the ordinary, I am reminded of its power. My appetite talks my stomach into sending fraudulent messages of acute hunger to my brain, when I know for a fact that I am not really hungry at all, that I have had plenty of nourishment today. But I *feel* hungry, enormously deprived—of something of which I have absolutely no actual need.

This is the real challenge of fasting: not just to abstain, but to move through the feelings of deprivation and need into the gift of it. To come to see God's power at work in my own body and spirit—the power that makes me able to say no to myself if I have decided to say no. This is pure gift. Saying no to myself with a peaceful spirit is not within my power. But it is not beyond God. And, in this little laboratory of God's love on the Fridays of Lent, I am given a taste of God's power to protect me from other things I might find myself drawn to in the course of my life—other things that really might hurt me, more than a piece of pie ever would.

Probably I could find a way to grit my teeth and abstain from food on my own. But only God can give me the power to relax and let go of it with joy and gratitude.

Saturday after Ash Wednesday

Remember, Lord, though frail we be, in your own image were we made.
HYMN 146, ATTRIBUTED TO GREGORY THE GREAT (540–604)

I refuse to have a hide-a-bed in my office. I don't want to make it easy or tempting to spend the night there: I want to go home at night. But there are nights when I must be there late and know I must return early in the morning. So now and then I find myself making a bed on the floor.

My office faces the street. I lie on the floor, grateful for the hard wood's disciplining of my weak back, and listen to Hell's Kitchen outside my window. Into the early hours of the morning, right up to the first graying of the black night, it never stops: people walking back and forth, laughing together as they return from the theaters. As the hours wear on, the theater people are safe at home. I hear other workers as I drift in and out of fitful sleep: prostitutes arguing with one another, with customers, with policemen. Loud voices raised in anger or in drunkenness. The occasional breaking of a bottle, the overturning of a trash can. A few nights ago, I remember uneasily, a man was stabbed on the corner of Ninth Avenue and 46th Street.

When light comes, I open the front door and look out. The street is quieter now than it ever is. Still, one exhausted woman across the street walks back and forth in front of the iron fence and waits for cars to pass. Perhaps one of them will slow and stop. Perhaps it will not be an undercover cop. Perhaps it will yield an encounter from which she can emerge with ten dollars or so. Her face is gray and rutted with deep lines. It is a hard face, but I can see that it is a beautiful one, and still young. She carries so much death in her body—the deadly grip of her drug addiction, the deadly cells of any number of diseases, the deadness of the act of love repeated again and again where there is no love—that it is hard to see the image of God there.

A car passes. She waves and smiles—an automatic gesture, but her smile is unexpectedly sweet. It is the smile of welcome, of a girl greeting the return of her sweetheart, of a child greeting her mother, a tentative smile of hope. It is the smile of my own little girls: waving good-bye to me from the front window as I drive off to work, catching sight of me in the train station and waving, waiting for me in the car at the end of the day, smiling and waving when I finally appear. That hopeful smile. The car slows and stops. The driver leans across the seat and opens the door. Expressionless, the young woman gets in.

Tonight I will not sleep here. Tonight I will go home, walk the broad, quiet streets to our house, with its soft, golden lights in the windows. My husband will look up from his book when I open the door. That hopeful smile.

The First Sunday of Lent

Now quit your care and anxious fear and worry;
for schemes are vain and fretting brings no gain.
HYMN 145, PERCY DEARMER (1867–1936)

"Sufficient unto the day is the evil thereof," Jesus used to say. "One day at a time," the people in recovery from addiction say, and it amounts to the same thing: In order to have a peaceful spirit, you need to live in the present, not in a future that has not yet happened or in a past about which you can do nothing. Today, like its predecessors, will last twenty-four hours. After that, it will be gone. So this is your only shot.

I knew a woman who had been abused as a child. This left her afraid of almost everything: of enclosed spaces, elevators, computers, germs, and almost all other people. Her world became an ever-smaller and ever-more-fragile circle of safety. Avoidance of danger was, for her, a full-time job. She literally had no life apart from seeing to it that bad things didn't happen to her.

Of course, she was profoundly emotionally disturbed. But many people who aren't disturbed still know something of this: Many people structure major parts of their lives around the avoidance of something that has hurt them in the past, depriving themselves of any number of opportunities for joy in the present. People who will never love again because love has hurt them before. People who will never try because they have known failure. People who will never play because they might lose.

This brings us to that very common Lenten fallacy: the idea that avoidance of things outside ourselves will protect us from evil. Lenten fasts and disciplines are not about warding off evil. Lent is not about locating danger outside of ourselves—that's neurosis, not Lent. It is about strengthening ourselves to live well in the world God has prepared for us, so that we may enjoy it as God has intended us to enjoy it.

It's a good world. Sometimes we misuse its goodness and get hurt, or someone else misuses it and we are caught in the line of fire. And sometimes we just find ourselves in the wrong place at the wrong time, through no fault of our own. So life can be dangerous: good and dangerous at the same time. We sample its goodness only by accepting its risks, accepting as our Lord and Savior the one who redeemed us—not by hiding from the world or by investing prudently in a 401-K plan, but by spending his very life. A life that was full of goodness and friendship and love, a life he clearly enjoyed.

Don't worry about saving yourself. You can't. It will all be over soon enough. You will be spent, you and your money and all your security and safety. All spent. Spend yourself, then, on something worth the price of you.

Creator of the earth and skies, to whom the words of life belong...
 HYMN 148, DAVID W. HUGHES (1911–1967)

When the Explorer landed with a gratifying soft thump on the surface of Mars, we all got to watch as it sent forth a robot to nose around and see what it could see. I, for one, had trouble with the scale of those video transmissions: Just how large *were* those rocks? Were we looking at mountains, or just at rocks of a size you could hold in your hand? It was not until I got a look at the robot itself—it was little, only about a foot long—that I could get a handle on the Martian land-scape. By then, I had already moved on to the bigger news from the red planet: that some of those rocks gave evidence of life having existed. Life on Mars! People my age, whose childhoods were peopled by space aliens on TV, cannot help but warm to the idea, even if it turns out that whatever Explorer found on Mars has been dead for billions of years and seems not to have been livelier than a mushroom.

We used to look up at the sky and wonder who was out there. The ancients did, too, ascribing intelligence and agency to the stars themselves. Intervention in human affairs, also, and that belief did not end with the Bronze Age: I know college graduates who firmly believe that the arrangement of stars and planets on the day they were born determines who they should and shouldn't date.

Faith in things like astrology is oddly poignant: people convinced that the heavens are as fascinated with us as we are with ourselves. Unable to believe that randomness plays as large a part in what happens to us as it manifestly does. Unable to rest in the uneasy truth: that there is no magic key to the future, no crystal ball. That we live in the midst of a mystery, and we won't know just what it all meant until its over. I can understand why a person would want to have Mars and Jupiter take over and handle things. I just don't think it happens.

Did Jesus know exactly what was going to happen to him, and how? I suspect that he did not. I am sorry if that idea offends you, but it is my belief. Truly human and truly divine, he was: truly human, learning the way humans learn— from experience. He knew that the powers of this world are strong, and that not all of them are benign. And he knew that life is larger than what we see here. The rest was revealed to him. It is his power that has revealed it to us.

Tuesday in Lent I

We have not known you: to the skies our monuments of folly soar,
and all our self-wrought miseries have made us trust ourselves the more.
HYMN 148, DAVID W. HUGHES (1911–1967)

The neighborhood is in an uproar: Fabulously wealthy real-estate developers want to change the zoning designation here so they can put up skyscrapers. We don't have buildings higher than six stories in this part of the city. It's one of only a few neighborhoods that have not been taken over by enormous towers, upended egg cartons that block the sun, making every side street look like evening in the early afternoon. It's also one of very few places in Manhattan where the working poor can still afford to live.

People are meeting two and three nights a week to plan the resistance. Politicians visit the Block Association, leaving behind unconvincing assurances of unspecified assistance. The developers promise all manner of benefits we will enjoy: There will be a special fund, they say, to aid struggling actors and struggling Off-Broadway theaters. Like St. Clement's, for instance. I suppose there could come a time when a developer comes knocking at our door with a little something to help us make up our minds.

Its says in the paper this morning that the mayor would like to reclaim all the little vest-pocket gardens that people have made out of vacant lots. Take those lots and sell them—developers would pay the city a lot of money for those lots. I go out and take a look at the one on 48th Street—a few crocuses have poked their heads up, I see, and will bloom in a couple of weeks. I remember how lovely it is in midsummer, how carefully the people husband its flowers and little hedges, how resolutely the bees buzz on their commute between blossom and beehive, how nice it is to sit in that little bit of soft green amid all the concrete and read a book. The mayor says that we have city parks we can go to. That's true. But these little gardens are gardens the people have made themselves, little gifts of God helped along by willing human hands. Money isn't everything.

Wednesday in Lent 1

...toward your presence bent: far off yet here—the goal of all desire.
HYMN 149, THOMAS H. CAIN (B. 1931)

I don't know why I said I would do three different conferences in three different parts of the country in four days. Somehow it sounded doable and even fun at the time. Just not thinking, I guess. Now I am almost at the end, my suitcase, replenished with some new little bottles of hotel shampoo and almond-smelling moisturizer, wedged tightly under the seat in front of me. The conferences were good. The people were great. I always end up enjoying these things. But the three hotel rooms were all alike, except for the one that smelled illicitly of cigarettes. The hotel restaurants were unmemorable, the conference banquets rubber chickens—there had been no time to consult the locals about seeking out better food.

I can hardly wait to get home. It glows in my imagination, lovelier than it really is—cleaner, anyway. My imaginary husband is there, gladder to see me than the real one may be. All the mail waiting is personal—no form appeals or credit card inducements, no glossy ads for menopause vitamins, replete with pictures of fresh-looking women allegedly my age. Real mail. I can hardly wait to get back to St. Clement's, also easier to come home to in imagination than it probably will be when I get there.

Business travel isn't all fun, even travel you said you wanted to do for a career you love. Home isn't always golden, either, even the home you have lovingly made for the people you love. Yet we continue to desire whatever it is we're missing, and to imagine it as lovelier than it is. Wherever we are, we want to be somewhere else.

So the presence of God is "far off yet here," eh? I guess that means that we take God, as we take ourselves, wherever we go. And that God's presence can redeem the tedium of our chronic unfulfillment, if we will allow it. That there can be wonder wherever we are, in whatever circumstances—the love of God, even in places where love looks pretty scarce. Because, although the places of our lives may be less lovely than we imagine them, they are also more holy than they appear.

Thursday in Lent I

If dead in you, so in you we arise...
HYMN 149, THOMAS H. CAIN (B. 1931)

Christopher Brian was fifteen months old when he died. He hadn't been feeling well for a day or two, and had just started some antibiotic for what looked like a fairly routine infection. But not much had been routine for Christopher in his young life. He had very little vision and impaired large muscle control. He couldn't talk. It was not yet clear how profound his mental retardation would be, but it was likely that there would be some.

At the funeral home, his tiny coffin was open. He lay on the fluffy white satin in a collegiate-looking sleeveless vest and a little shirt: a little man. Perfect skin, perfect long eyelashes, perfect golden curls, little perfect hands. He looked to be asleep. His Winnie-the-Pooh was with him, and another bear: friends from the beginning.

There was also a snapshot of him, mouth wide open in a happy baby grin. Total delight suffused the little face. The photograph shouted with life, while the little subject who lay beside it was absolutely still. There will be no more big grins, no more laughs, no more cuddles. There will also be no more worry, no more questions, no more discouragements. It was crystal clear, though, as his grieving parents received whispered comfort from their friends and family, that all the worry and discouragement in the world was worth it just for the sake of having Christopher. As big a job as it was caring for a child with such special needs, nobody there thought it would have been better for him not to have been.

He was in Christ, the priest said in the homily—the same priest who had baptized him not too long before. The gift of life came from God, and now Christopher was returning to God. Christopher never got a chance to understand much about Christianity. He never got to make mistakes and pay for them, never got to know what forgiveness is. There was a lot he didn't know—most things, I guess. But none of that had anything to do with his being in Christ. The most erudite of theologians is on no better footing than Christopher where the love of God is concerned. Looking at the little face in the picture, so full of the happiness of that moment, we knew that this is what his life is like now. Eternal delight, unfettered by weakness or pain. Life with the One who gave him life, first here on earth and then life without end in another place.

Friday in Lent I

If thou rememberest every sin,
if nought but just reward we win,
could we abide thy presence?

HYMN 151, MARTIN LUTHER (1483–1546)

"Too bad you can't work your way to heaven," I say to Clarence.

"We'd be there already, I know that much," he says, filling a big pot half full of sudsy water and beginning to scrub. The Sunday night supper after Actors' Vespers is over, and I'm fading fast. "You go on," he says, "I'll get this." *Where does he get his energy,* I wonder. I feel I should stay and help, but I take him up on his offer and make my way slowly to my office. It looks like the shop of a demented costume designer, as usual: Watty's Palestinian caftan, which he wore as Joseph in the Epiphany pageant, is back from the cleaners, along with my long black *capa nigra,* used this year to envelope Susan's wicked King Herod. *Richard III's* deformity hangs on the wall: a tan spandex body suit with padding sewn into the back to create a frighteningly realistic hump. A hopelessly smashed typewriter hangs next to it: a prop from Sam Shepard's *True West,* whose writer protagonist took out his frustration on the thing night after night with a golf club. Papers are everywhere: service bulletins, sheets of music, unanswered letters, a form letter from the bishop wanting to know when he should make his annual visitation to St. Clement's.

So much work. So little time. So few resources. So much exhaustion. I wonder, as I begin to push papers around the desk in an ineffectual effort to bring order out of some of the chaos, if all this work is somehow an attempt on my part to do what I know can't be done: to earn the love of God. Or the love of people. Or, perhaps, my own self-love. When will I ever have done enough? Probably never.

Justice is not the same thing as the love of God. Justice is what measures the human scale of right and wrong, that which prevents us from misusing each other—or, at least, lets us know when we have done so. God's love is different: It is free, not calculated from what we have done, or left undone. God just loves us, inadequacies and all.

By all means, work hard, if that for which you labor is important to you and those you love. But do not think you earn your place in God's heart that way. And do not think that you lose it if you fail to measure up. You already have a place in God's heart, and you can never lose it.

Saturday in Lent I

Forty days and forty nights thou wast fasting in the wild;
forty days and forty nights tempted, and yet undefiled.
HYMN 150, GEORGE HUNT SMYTTAN (1822–1870)

Forty days and forty nights—we've heard that before, yes? The rain that became Noah's flood lasted exactly that long. And the children of Israel wandered in the wilderness for how long? For forty years. And now the temptation of Jesus is right on schedule, too, lasting exactly forty days and forty nights. What a coincidence.

"Forty days and forty nights" is just Bible-ese for "a really long time." An unusually long time, it means—a longer time than a person would normally expect for the phenomenon in question. The biblical writers weren't very precise about measuring time. We are, though: Our wrist watches have second hands on them, and our Olympic runners divide their precious seconds into ten tiny pieces of time.

I read somewhere that a reporter asked a few dozen New Yorkers if they could guess what time it was without looking at their watches, and more than two-thirds of them got within five minutes of the actual time. We're good. So it makes some of us a little uncomfortable to consider the possibility that they weren't—that the precision so important to modern people was not of much interest to the people who wrote the texts we consider sacred and authoritative for the conduct of our lives. If the flood really didn't last forty days and forty nights after all, we think edgily, what else in the Bible might be somewhat overstated?

Probably lots of things. Only some of Scripture is history in the journalistic sense we employ when we use the term "history" today. The rest is poetry, myth, law—there's a lot in that collection of ancient books. So we don't pick up our Bibles the way we might pick up our almanacs. We read them for other kinds of truth—for how to know God's continuing presence in lives that do contain long, humdrum stretches of time in which the more vivid evidences of the divine love are a tad scarce. We are tempted to behave as if God were far away. We go for days, weeks—forty days and forty nights—without a sign. But God always acts, even if the children of Israel have to wait. Even if Jesus has to struggle with temptation in the desert. It may rain for forty days and forty nights, but it doesn't rain forever.

The Second Sunday of Lent

Make clear, make clear,
make clear where truth and light appear.
<small>HYMN 145, PERCY DEARMER (1867–1936)</small>

"Do you think it endangers a person's religious faith to explore other religions?" This was the question of the month. I am on a panel of clergy that is consulted, occasionally, by a women's magazine for opinions on questions about spirituality.

"Well, no," I answer, "I don't think so at all." I go on to talk about there being more than one path to truth, about God's presence throughout the whole of humanity and the whole of creation. I say that we can trust ourselves to experience the world and learn from it, and that doubts and questions are a very important part of faith. I tell her about Pamela's Monday night Christian yoga class at St. Clement's.

A fact-checker calls me back in a few days. "Let's see, you said, 'All religions are equally true,' right?" Well, not exactly. Certainly one that told its adherents to lie down and suffocate themselves with plastic bags over their heads so that they all could fly to a comet is not a faith that should be encouraged. There's nothing true or lovely about religious practices that hurt people. It's not narrow-minded to object to such things. Religious pluralism does not demand this.

"No, I said there are *many paths*," I tell her patiently, and give the example of the people with the plastic bags over their heads. I hear her computer keys click softly as she corrects her copy. I think of the magazine's readers—twenty-five- to forty-year-old women who like fashion and self-improvement and who worry a lot about their figures. Freedom to think for themselves is important to young people—it's important to all people. One rabbi on the panel was a little less expansive than I was about sampling other cultures' truths—but then, six million Episcopalians weren't slaughtered over a five-year period in an attempt to eradicate them. I bet I'd feel more protective if they had been.

But still: If it is true, it is of God. Wherever it arose.

Monday in Lent II

The covenant, so long revealed to those of faith in former time,
Christ by his own example sealed, the Lord of love, in love sublime.
HYMN 146, ATTRIBUTED TO GREGORY THE GREAT (540–604)

Apparently, there is now a new kind of human being. We are digitized now, seconds away from electronic contact with people we've never met and never will meet face-to-face. Any fact ever known is a few keystrokes away. I have heard that soon there may be no such thing as a book.

Kids are now born knowing all about the Internet. Some of us who are not kids are learning about it. And some of us learn about it and then forget, so we keep having to start over. We know we are on our way to the scrap heap. We will co-exist uncomfortably with the new humans, the way Neanderthals and Cro-Magnons did for a few years. But we will be no match for them. History moves only forward.

But consider: More than half of the world's population has never made a telephone call. Bet you ten dollars they don't have laptops. And there are Luddites among us in the First World, too: people fully capable of logging on and, for all I know, of beaming up, but who choose not to play. The Unabomber was one, and on days when I'm tired and cranky, I am one.

Christ completed the old covenant, and now we're a new creation in Christ, says St. Paul. Why do we think that was nothing but good news to the people who first heard it? It's *scary* to be presented with something radically new. To be told that henceforth life is going to be nothing at all like it was is alarming. It doesn't surprise me that people didn't just embrace the Christ event with easy, open arms, that Mary and Joseph were perplexed (which is probably putting it mildly), that the first Christians hid away in an upper room and didn't talk to anybody for days.

The Internet is really easy once you know how to use it, I am told. "User-friendly" is the term. I can sometimes grope my way around it and end up with some information I need, although I can't yet do it faster than it would take just to pick up the phone and call someone. I am not yet a new kind of human being.

Until I am, I will be suspicious of the new, impatient with it. It will seem to me like a lot of work for very little return.

Life in Christ looked like that at the outset. Still does, from the outside. Lots of work and self-denial and suspension of rationality for some incomprehensible promises of a larger life nobody really knows anything about. No wonder not everybody signs on. The old creation doesn't get it. In Christ, we are part of the new.

Tuesday in Lent II

Should not we thy sorrow share?

HYMN 150, GEORGE HUNT SMYTTAN (1822–1870)

"Jesus *had* to be crucified," the young man explains to me earnestly. We are on a plane, and he has been witnessing to me since we left Newark. I look out the window, hoping that the body of water below us is Lake Michigan. "Because crucifixion is the worst kind of death anyone has ever endured."

Is it? What about mustard gas, I wonder to myself. What about the electric chair? What about emphysema? Crucifixion is a terrible way to go, but so are a lot of other ways. None of them is any great honor. Dying is a terrible thing. Is the death of Jesus really about topping all other forms of human suffering? Is his saving gift to us really the fact that he suffered more than we suffer? Or is it something else?

What saves us about Jesus' sacrifice is that he joins us in what we must also endure. "None of us is getting out of here alive," our neighbor Orry used to joke.

May he rest in peace, dead at fifty-two of pancreatic cancer, which was also not a day at the beach. Death is in all of our futures—it was even in the future of the Son of God, living among human beings. In Christ, God forever closes the chasm between heaven and earth. Henceforth, nothing human is foreign to God, and no human sorrow separates us from the love of God. Not even our great fear: the end of earthly life.

We fear it profoundly. We can scarcely bring ourselves to think about our own end. Only rarely do we allow ourselves to wonder by what means death will come to us, and even then we cannot think about it for very long. Human beings are not built to look death in the face for long stretches of time. We need to feel our own continuation. Even those who know themselves to be facing death soon have moments in which they allow themselves to deny its reality. They need such moments, little breaks from a frightening truth.

We want our Jesus to have been a superman of some sort, to have been unnaturally good and bright as a child, to have lived life in a superhuman way. The church has not taught this. Jesus was not superman. His death was not a megadeath. It was a human death, like ours, soaked in sorrow and betrayal and defeat. Truly human, he tasted our despair. Truly God, he redeems it.

Wednesday in Lent II

Then if Satan on us press,
Jesus, Savior, hear our call!

HYMN 150, GEORGE HUNT SMYTTAN (1822–1870)

My one o'clock appointment is late. Maybe I can make some sense of the mare's nest on my desk. I begin, pitching notices of meetings that have already occurred and ads for new styles of church offering envelopes. I pick up a piece of scratch paper to see if it's a keeper. "Don't react!" is scrawled all over the sheet, again and again, twenty or thirty times. It's my handwriting.

Some people make me angry. I need to try my best to respond to them with self-control. I need not to rise to the bait of their behavior with angry behavior of my own. This is hard for me. "Don't react!" I write on whatever old envelope comes to hand. Don't react. Remain your own master. Don't let someone else control you. Control yourself.

I suppose Satan would prefer that I lose my temper. He certainly tries to bring that about, and sometimes he succeeds. I feel my heart pounding and my voice tightening. Sometimes my head hurts. After all these years of ministry, I do not cease to be amazed at the ease with which he can walk in and take charge.

But I belong to Christ. It is to Christ that I have entrusted my life. While Satan is stronger than I am, Christ is stronger than he is. Stronger than my anger. Able to still the pounding of my heart and, furthermore, able to soften it. Is the person before me only a child of God when he is being sweet and generous? No—he's a child of God all the time. Does God love him only when he is good? No—God just loves him. Somewhere within him the image of God is visible, and God is abundantly able to help me see it.

Thursday in Lent II

And as through stony ground the green shoots break,
glorious in springtime dress of leaf and flower...
HYMN 149, THOMAS H. CAIN (B. 1931)

There are daffodils at the Korean fruit and vegetable stand today, pots and pots of them. Brave yellow starry blossoms and tight buds, promising more stars. Somebody said there would be more snow tonight, and the gray-white sky suggests the likelihood. The buildings, the sidewalk, the sky: They are all gray. I am wearing a gray coat. Enough: I stop and buy a little pot of the daffodils to put in the lobby of St. Clement's.

We make the city. Almost everything in it is made by human means. Made by machines, made of concrete, made anonymously and used anonymously. Most things in the city are hard: Asphalt is hard, concrete is hard, stone and steel are hard. Cold and hard. Our faces are hard, as we hurry along the sidewalks under the gray sky.

The daffodils are soft. They'll break, if you're not careful—the blossoms will break off. They are not gray. They are the color of the sun that makes them possible. Soon there will be other colors, and they will not just be at the fruit stands: Relatives of the daffodils will peek unexpectedly amid the hardness, in boxes in front of apartment buildings, in window boxes five flights up. People will help the color and softness come among them. Soon the sky will turn blue and soften. Soon I will leave my coat at home.

For many ancient peoples, this annual softening was all the God they needed. Our resurrection hope took its place alongside older ones, all based on the return of spring after the hardness of winter. And yet ours is not only that ancient hope: In Christ the seasons and times are contained, and Christ is beyond them. The entry of Christ Jesus into human existence is an entry into the seasons for the sake of those whose lives they determine. He enters our seasons with a message: This is life and this is death, but this is not all there is to life and death. He comes that you might have life beyond what you observe and what you know.

Friday in Lent II

So shall we have peace divine.
HYMN 150, GEORGE HUNT SMYTTAN (1822–1970)

Imagine: Spirituality is fashionable. In a development that nobody could have predicted, the best-seller lists are full of books about God, life after death, and the separation of church and state. *Time* magazine has noted that when its issues have images of Jesus, Mary, Moses, or an angel on the cover, they outsell the normal run by several hundred thousand copies. Clearly, we all want to read about these things—the way we all wanted to read about Inner Tennis ten or fifteen years ago.

Is that all it is? Is the new interest in spiritual things just a logical outgrowth of the fitness movement, the soul's trendy equivalent of oat bran and Stairmaster? Certainly that's part of it, and it would account for the focus on self upon which many pop spiritual paths build: an endless, ageless, wrinkleless body, and an endless, ageless, mistakeless mind. *Of course* you want to meditate: It improves your workout and lowers your stress, and maybe even your cholesterol. It's good for you.

And if what we're talking about is just lighting a few candles, playing soft music, and visualizing waterfalls, "good for you" is about as far as you need to go. Something happens to many people, though, once they start down the path of contemplation, no matter how self-absorbed a motive may have caused them to begin: They begin to sense the existence of a dimension of life that they had not known existed before. It is reached by a path that begins within them, but they know it to be other than just themselves. It is not easily described to another person. It is uniquely experienced by each of us, but it is much more than "my true self" or "my essence." It is a hint of God.

It is rare for a human being ever to get more than a hint. You don't get them every day. But a hint is more than enough—we are talking about something powerful enough to cause and contain the universe, yet gentle enough to turn the human soul inside out without killing it. "Humankind cannot bear very much reality," T.S. Eliot said, and it is so. You can't order in a spiritual life the way you would a pizza; it is too potent a thing to be treated so casually. But the repeated discipline of waiting upon God puts the soul in the way of these hints of God.

Saturday in Lent II

Spare us, O Lord, who now confess
our sins and all our wickedness,
and, for the glory of thy Name,
our weakened souls to health reclaim.

HYMN 152, ATTRIBUTED TO GREGORY THE GREAT (540–604)

So much in our tradition depends on our sinfulness, an emphasis almost completely mystifying and more than a little off-putting to our secular friends, to whom it just looks neurotic. That is probably because they misunderstand what we understand the effect of sin to be. We don't think human sin sets us apart in a state of shame, like Hester Prynne in *The Scarlet Letter*. The question we ask about a person is not, Is she a sinner?—for we know she is. Everybody is. The question we ask is, Which sin holds her back from the fullness of joy for which God made her? What needs healing?

Most people making a first confession are scared to death. Things hidden from view for years are about to be shared with another human being and with God. I point out that God has already known about these things for some time, and then I share my own experience with getting something off my chest. What usually happens is that the Great Shameful Secret, once it's on the table, doesn't look nearly as powerful as it did behind closed doors. *I did that. I wish I hadn't. I regret it and wish with all my heart it hadn't happened*. Well, okay! That wasn't so terrible. The person who just confessed almost always feels freer, as she should: She's just joined the human race, a family from which she was formerly cut off because she had walked away with the mistaken belief that her sin separated her from everybody else and made her unworthy to be among them. But it doesn't. She has a planet full of brothers and sisters who have also made bad choices from time to time and also regret them.

Forgiveness is real. It can set you free. Asking for it is not nearly as hard as almost everyone thinks it will be.

The Third Sunday of Lent

Speak to our souls the quickening word, and turn our darkness into day.
HYMN 148, DAVID W. HUGHES (1911–1967)

It is dark, cold; we are tired and overscheduled. It seems that the church school needs a new curriculum, that a capital campaign is in order. Perhaps there is still time, before the millennium turns, for one of the shiny new evangelism programs. The flu season was early and its bug virulent this year: We have experienced this as a personal affront. Meanwhile, we have begun to wonder if our preaching is all that it once was: In the middle of an anecdote, the dreadful suspicion that we have told this story before grips us. The people shake our hands and tell us that this morning's message was very inspiring. The feeling of dread is not dispelled.

Understanding that physical exercise is an antidote to stress, we creep out of bed very early so as not to awaken our sleeping spouse. We go to the gym, where we walk on moving paths to nowhere, climb moving stairs to go nowhere, and furiously pedal on stationary bicycles to nowhere. We try not to allegorize this.

And yet a young man comes in to talk about the possibility that he is being called to priesthood. We find ourselves remembering that tentative era in our own lives, remembering the momentousness of every step: the first time we told someone else about our calling, the day we started seminary, the first time we saw ourselves in a clerical collar, what it was like to interview with the Commission on Ministry, with the bishop, with the search committee. We listen to the young man tell us what he loves and what he fears. We recall that we loved and feared some of the same things. "Why don't you meditate on the liturgy for ordination," we tell him. "Spend a little time with it every day, and let's talk again in a month or so." When he leaves we lean back in our chairs and realize that the conversation has left us energized.

We are busy. Our task is huge, much larger than we are. It is easy to forget, in our busyness, that none of our gifts and powers come from us. None of our successes. And none of our failures sum up our ministries. Our ministries are simply not about our own power. The strength we summon to do God's work is not our strength: It comes to us from God. And so we will find the strength. There will be a way to serve God in the church without becoming exhausted and dwelling in self-pity. God will use us as we are and supply in us what we are not. We walk the walk toward human powerlessness once again, the stripping away of our pretensions to omnicompetence: Jesus' walk toward the ultimate human powerlessness. We remember again—how is it that we keep forgetting?—that it was in his surrender to this human truth that he beat down death under his feet. The power of God comes mightily upon the tired limits of our strength: It is, perhaps, in the humbling public living of this repeated empowering that the ordained lead most gracefully.

Your love, O Lord, our sinful race has not returned, but falsified.
<small>HYMN 146, ATTRIBUTED TO GREGORY THE GREAT (540–604)</small>

Have we "falsified" God's love? Have we transmitted it through the generations as something other than what it is? We must have, since there are so many people who grew up going to church but still don't know that God loves them. So many people who say they believe in God but not in "organized religion." (I guess they've never been to St. Clement's, which would definitely be *dis*organized religion!) So many Christians who are convinced that God hates the people they hate.

So how can we go about learning to "return" the love of God? It would be unreasonable to ask someone to love God without first coming to know of God's love through the loving people of God. If we are to understand that God gave us his Son, even though we have some really nasty habits—in fact, that this happened precisely *because* we are that way, and hence in great need of the divine love—then it makes no sense at all for us to show love selectively. Absolutely everyone must be welcomed. We can't show forth a loving God if we ourselves are not loving.

If we were loving, though, we'd miss out on the enthralling and ancient human pastime of sorting our brothers and sisters into in-groups and out-groups. Nothing makes us feel better quicker than to say someone else is worse than we are, and we would be denied that seductive quick fix to our egos if we decided to make love our reflex instead of judgment. But judgment never makes us feel good for long: It's like a sugar high, gone as quickly as it came, leaving us unsatisfied again. Love is different. God is love, so godly human love is eternal—one of the very few things about us that will last.

Tuesday in Lent III

We have not loved you: far and wide
the wreckage of our hatred spreads,
and evils wrought by human pride
recoil on unrepentant heads.

HYMN 148, DAVID W. HUGHES (1911–1967)

I saw in the newspaper that one of the men who was convicted of personal responsibility for and involvement in terrible atrocities during the Bosnian war hung himself yesterday in his jail cell. He disabled the emergency light in his corridor and ended his life in the dark: he hung himself from the hinge of his cell door. There was a picture of him during his trial: husky, young, and handsome, with a droopy mustache and a fine head of hair.

He had been unrepentant during the trial. That, and the abundance of evidence against him, made his war crimes conviction a relatively easy matter. I wonder what it was that got to him, there in his cell, day after day. Was it lately born compassion for his victims—hundreds of Croatian men, forced to run a gauntlet of bayonets and pistol shots and then mowed down into a mass grave? Or was it despair over the prospect of a life behind bars? Had his family turned their backs on him in shame? Or did he wish to preempt retaliation from other prisoners taking justice into their own hands? Now no one will ever know.

I wonder if he knew anything about forgiveness? Certainly, he had shown none in his terrible crimes. Was there anyone in the jail who could have helped him take hold of redemption? Anyone in his family who would have helped lift the eyes of his spirit from the devilish equations that demand fresh blood for ancient injury, keeping hatred alive and dormant for centuries, ready to burst malignantly into flame? Or did he die as he had lived, full of a hatred so venomous that it could murder many times?

And what happens to him now? Suicides, in his culture, are excluded from the faithful even in death—they are not buried in the general cemetery with everybody else. His isolated body will, as long as the earth endures, bespeak his soul's earthly aloneness. But God also loves those who commit terrible crimes. Christ also redeems them. The Holy Spirit also heals them. Now, in eternal life, as he never could in earthly life, he rests in peace.

Wednesday in Lent III

***Wilt thou forgive that sin, by which I won
others to sin, and made my sin their door?***

HYMN 141, JOHN DONNE (1573–1631)

Gossip is a sin like that. Gossip partnerships can develop—friendships whose only bond is a mutual dislike of a third party. Not a pretty sight.

"I feel terrible telling you this behind her back," the young woman says miserably. She is almost in tears. She has a painful issue with a friend, and she wants some help in understanding it. But she feels like she is telling tales out of school, and it's a terrible feeling.

Now, that's not gossip. How are you ever going to get help if you can't talk about what's wrong? There's no salacious pleasure in this conversation—the young woman is miserable. This is an utterly appropriate reaching out for a shoulder to lean on and a listening ear. This is a conversation about how best to remain in a relationship of love and mutual respect. Gossip is a conversation that happens only because that relationship is broken, or very nearly so.

And yet, even such anguished reaching out needs to be monitored. The relief one gets from sharing is a powerful thing, and a welcome change from the anger and hurt that drove the young woman to speak in the first place. She'll feel better after this talk. Her heart will remember that relief and may hanker after it again. Her heart talking to me about her friend so that she can take steps to confront their problems and heal them. However, in some cases it may feel so good to vent that the harder work of self-examination goes undone.

So even a good thing can open the way to something hurtful. Moral life is a delicate thing, a mix of self-love and selflessness, always seeking a balance that sometimes eludes us.

Thursday in Lent III

So Daniel trained his mystic sight, delivered from the lions' might.
HYMN 143, LATIN, 6TH CENTURY, TRANSLATED BY MAURICE F. BELL (1862–1947)

A miracle. God reveals his might in this well-known story of the young man spending the night among hungry lions as if they were sleepy house cats.

"So where's *my* miracle?" someone asks. Someone who could really use one. "Why did Daniel, or Elijah, or all those other people in the Bible, or those people I've read about in the tabloids at the supermarket checkout counter, get a miracle and I'm left with my suffering?" It's a rare person who has not asked this question when visited by suffering. And it's a question that has no satisfactory answer: The responses that people of faith have often given leave many sufferers trembling with anger. *God is punishing me for something I've done wrong. God is testing my faith. God is teaching me a lesson. God doesn't send you anything you can't handle.*

They are well mannered, these stock answers to that ancient anguished cry, and they do get God off the hook, but they do not ring quite true. God needs to torture us to test us? Can't think of any other way to instruct us? That doesn't sound like the God who could create a universe out of love. Does God really need to be gotten off the hook? Does God need such a vigorous public-relations effort from us, so anxious a tap dance of reasons why bad things are really good things? Bad things aren't good; they're bad. The silver lining in your cloud doesn't make it something other than a cloud. Most twelve-year-olds are too smart to be fooled by commercials for God's goodness that depend on denying the evidence of our own eyes, the experience of our own hearts.

I think "Why?" is really the wrong question. "What?" is far better, a question put at the end of pain rather than at its beginning. "Why?" focuses on the past and on myself. It locates me at the center of a universe that is all about me, and that is not the truth. The universe really isn't all about me. Microbes aren't appointed by God to speed to my door and teach me a lesson. They're just living out their microscopic lives and happen upon me in their path. The out-of-control Chevy on a dark road isn't intended to test my faith. These things just happen, like it says on those bumper stickers.

But what can happen because of these things? They may not be intended to teach me, but I will assuredly learn from them if I allow myself to learn. They may not be purposed to punish me, but I can certainly repent in the midst of them, turn my life around because I have been brought face-to-face with the truth of just how fragile it really is. We will not be able to avoid suffering in this life; we wear crosses around our necks to remind us that the Christ through whom all things were made did not avoid it. If I focus on the possibility of meaning in the midst of suffering and not on its intention, I find there the God who graciously holds the future in one hand and the past in the other. And there is no limit to the love I can know because I have found that God.

Friday in Lent III

Led by your cloud by day, by night your fire...
   Hymn 149, Thomas H. Cain (b. 1931)

How to tell if a house is home to one or more adolescents? Swing by at night: If there are young folks in residence, every light in the house will be blazing. Cellar to attic. This is especially true if the parents are out for the evening. "Kids are wasteful," my husband says. Maybe. But I have another theory about this well-known phenomenon. I think young adults are scared of the dark.

I think they are on the edge between childhood and the daunting frontier of independence. The same teenagers who slam shut their bedroom doors after a confrontation, vowing never to set foot in your house again once they're eighteen, are also not at all sure they ever want to leave home. Back they come, from college or work or the army, filling the house again with noise and dirty laundry and filling the refrigerator with junk food. And, at night on these brief vacations, your house blazes with light, not the little pools of lamplight you employ while reading at night, but blazing as it did every night when they lived at home, every bulb shining as brightly as its wattage will allow.

Sanela came to us two years ago, when she was twenty-one. She is brilliant and beautiful, a serious student, a hard worker, mature far beyond her years. Her education in her native Bosnia was cruelly interrupted by the war: The University was in Sarajevo, firmly in Serbian hands, and a young Muslim woman could not hope to enroll. It seemed for a time that she would never be able to go to school. She felt as if her youth was passing her by. She had almost resigned herself to her disappointment when word came that there would be a place for her at Rutgers.

She lives with Q and me when she is not in the dorm. She is so much more serious than her American peers. So studious. So hungry for learning. She is ardent in her desire to rebuild her country after its years of suffering. We think she could probably do that single-handedly. She carries a heavy course load and is on the dean's list—for work done entirely in a language not her own. She works for the economics department. She speaks five languages. She is president of a national organization of foreign students studying in America. She volunteers with a troop of inner-city Girl Scouts. She is amazing.

She has seen people killed before her eyes. She has known young men from her high school imprisoned in concentration camp by other young men from her high school. She has taken shelter in subway tunnels during air raids and hit the ground in an open field under a hail of snipers' bullets. She has known hunger. She has lived for months at a time with little food and scarce water, and often no electricity.

We turn the corner and pull into our driveway. We know Sanela is home alone, waiting for us to return. We look at the house and smile at each other: Every light in the house is blazing. From cellar to attic.

Saturday in Lent III

For is not this the fast that I have chosen?
(The prophet spoke) To shatter every yoke,
of wickedness the grievous bands to loosen,
oppression put to flight.
    HYMN 145, PERCY DEARMER (1867–1936)

"I think I'm all cooked out," Clarence says ruefully. "I can't think of a thing to make for supper tonight."

We have a Sunday night supper for actors and their friends. It follows a vesper service in which we chant the ancient canticles and psalms and prayers, a simple pool of prayer and music that never fails to calm and center me at the end of a frantic Sunday.

"How about we just put some sandwich stuff out and let people make their own?" I ask. "They'll survive." Clarence agrees. We're both tired.

The people begin to filter in shortly before five. The actors who attend Actors' Sanctuary are probably not actors of whom you have heard. They are the yeomen of the New York theater community, the people who live from show to show and collect unemployment in between. They send out résumés and head shots by the hundred. They put themselves on the line at audition after audition. Many have supported themselves in this precarious way for decades. Many of the people who attend are not yet at the point in their careers where they command any salary at all. Sometimes it's just carfare. And often it's just nothing. When somebody gets a paying job—in any role in any play—everyone on Sunday night applauds.

They are weary. They work in offices and restaurants, as house painters and cleaning people and dog walkers. They sit quietly in the candlelight and sing the simple tunes. Some of them are singers as well. Some Sundays, we sound pretty good.

Are they oppressed by wickedness? There's no shortage of it in the theater industry, although nobody's putting a gun to their heads to make them stay in it. But they are the custodians of something indispensable to human culture: words, the beauty and power of them, and movement, its beauty and power, and human memory experienced corporately. Literature does that, too, but reading is something you do by yourself. Theater is community: You don't have it unless there's an audience. Just now the politicians are congratulating themselves because we no longer have a strong National Endowment for the Arts. We are the only developed country that doesn't. We are to understand this as progress.

Someone has said that the human being fully alive is the greatest glory of God. Who knows the extent of God's glories? Not me. But I do know that it is God's desire for each beloved child to live abundantly, as abundantly as he or she is able.

The Fourth Sunday of Lent

And thus my hope is in the Lord, and not in my own merit.
HYMN 151, MARTIN LUTHER (1483–1546)

I would walk slowly with my mother. She would hold onto my arm. We stopped often. I was strong. She was old.

June 2, 1992
I believe, before this happens, that there is nothing my will and my drive cannot accomplish. Some people are not strong enough to triumph over the bad things that happen to them, but I am. I simply will not allow myself to be weak.

I don't see the car before it hits me. I am walking along the sidewalk on a beautiful New York day in early summer, looking in the shop windows. I am thinking—that very second, imagine—about how fine a thing it is to live in New York and walk on these streets. I will look in the windows. I will get some exercise.

63

I will drop my manuscript off at the publishers. Then I will meet my husband and some friends for dinner. I am thinking—that very second—about how fine a thing it is to be me.

When it comes, it feels like somebody hitting me in the small of my back with a club. A Louisville slugger, hitting me hard. Roger Maris. Babe Ruth. A real professional. Or somebody who is mentally unbalanced. Or a mugger. I'm being mugged, I think with interest. This will be a new experience. I've never been mugged before. I am not afraid.

Very, very slowly, it seems—although this cannot really be true: All this is happening within a period of one second—I am nudged toward the brick wall of the building in whose windows I have been looking. Very, very slowly—but again, this cannot be true—I put up my hands to cushion the impact of flesh and bone on brick and cast iron. I claw at the flat faces of bricks. My ankle grinds into the edge of a cast iron step. I begin to sink sideways. How stupid. I hope no one has seen me behave so foolishly. I will just walk away now.

"Stop!" A man I do not know is running toward me. "Don't move!" Obediently, I do not move. I wonder if it would be all right to fall down, or would that be self-pitying grandstanding on my part? I think it would be. If I fall down, it will be an admission that something has happened and nothing has really happened. I begin to sink again, down to the sidewalk, nice leather purse and manila envelope still in my hands, thank goodness; I mustn't let go of these things. You don't leave your things unattended in New York.

But pain on the sidewalk. Pain when I am touched. Blinding pain when I am lifted. Pain in the ambulance. Pain and fear—"I'm falling," I hear my own voice wailing. "No, you're not. You're strapped in nice and tight," says the EMS person, kindly contradicting me. Pain in the emergency room, hours and hours, a day. A silver-haired lady in a pink smock brings me a pillow and smiles gently. She disappears. The pillow hurts. I must find somebody to take it away. I wet the bed. Two nurses change the sheets under me: When they roll me onto my side, I cover my face and cry. One of them comes to me later and says she is sorry. *That's all right.*

I can go home if I can walk. But when I try, one leg drags behind. "What am I supposed to do with this leg?" I ask people who pass by. Nobody seems to know. I hold onto my daughter's arm. She helps me try to walk several times. I fail each time. On my third try, she faints.

June 7, 1992

A doctor catches me dragging myself along the edge of my bed toward the bathroom. "I'll have you restrained if you try that again," he says, "and I'm not kidding."

"I had to use the toilet. I rang and rang, but nobody came."

"Just wet the bed, then. But don't get up."

June 8, 1992

"See that leg? Could you lift it up and move it a few inches over to the left? It's slipping off the bed." Bill picks up the leg and moves it. It is my leg, but I can't move it. So Bill moves it. He is a verger at Trinity Church. There he does things to make people feel welcome.

June 9, 1992

My daughter runs in to see me. She is double-parked; her sister has the kids in the car. She is all in white. She is like an angel. She is in a hurry. She just wanted to see that I was all right. She bends down to kiss me. She smells like flowers. I am surrounded by flowers.

June 11, 1992

I step on an artificial curb and back down. I do it again. I do it again. Your cane moves with your bad leg, but on the other side. I am doing well. The rehab is full of wheelchairs. I ride one there and back. But I walk, once I am there: a miniature world, like a miniature golf course. Steps leading nowhere, artificial curbs. Half a real car, to practice getting in and out: Sit down backwards first, then pick up your leg with your hand and put it in the car. I don't remember now how I did this before the accident.

June 13, 1992

The sun is bright outside. It is still summer. The cabs are still yellow. I get into one backwards, pick up my leg with my hand and bring it inside: This works. My first real car. Soon I will be taking cabs in to work. I will be back to work in less than a month. So I was right, then: Strength of will is all you need. You can't keep a strong woman down.

January 24, 1993

I was not right. I can't sit through dinner at night. I drag myself to bed. A man is following me down a dangerous hill. He comes closer. He touches me on my back. He is magic; his touch imparts pain. I beg him to stop. "Please take your hand away." He will not. "Please." He touches me more and more, and the touch drills into my back like an ice pick. I open my mouth to scream; thick syllables come out of it, wailing that awakens my husband. He soothes me in the dark. I take a pill. In the morning I am groggy and stupid.

April 16, 1993
"You should see this doctor I know."

September 23, 1993
"You should try acupuncture."

February 12, 1994
"You should take magnesium."

May 14, 1994
"You should take echinacea five times a day."

December 1, 1994
"You should bathe in salts from the Dead Sea."

March 14, 1995
"You should take antidepressant drugs."

July 20, 1995
I can't get up at five in the morning to write in luxurious solitude anymore. I can't run. I can't sleep on my side anymore. I can't lift much. I can't say that strength of personality ensures my triumph over any obstacle. I'm beginning to suspect that it has hardly anything to do with it.

My mother wasn't really old. She was only sixty-four when she died. I just thought she was old because I was young. And I wasn't really strong because of my will to be strong. I was just lucky.

Monday in Lent IV

I have a sin of fear that when I've spun
my last thread, I shall perish on the shore.
HYMN 141, JOHN DONNE (1573–1631)

Most of the people at the funeral sat on the aisle. At Trinity Church, that's a long walk: The family walked it—daughters, a sister, brothers, looking straight ahead. Evadne wasn't with them, even though it was her own mother's funeral. Instead, she came in at the front of the procession, swinging the censer and sending billows of fragrant smoke into the high vault of the ceiling. Trinity owns a number of expensive censers, but Evadne's choice was the large one, affectionately nicknamed "Big Bertha," whose size, shape, and perforations always guarantee the most smoke.

Of course Evadne was thurifer at her own mother's funeral. Her mother would have expected nothing else. Theirs was a family that expected to contribute, to serve rather than to be served. She had been a nurse for more than fifty years; her husband was a physician. People spoke: a woman who had worked on her floor for years, another who had served on the board of a homeless shelter with her, a middle-aged woman who remembered playing at their big house in Brooklyn, a center of learning and encouragement for all the kids in the neighborhood. "Who among us will ever forget the Zoo Club?" she asked, and several other middle-aged professionals in the congregation nodded and smiled at the memory.

"...and we commit her body to its final resting place: Earth to earth, ashes to ashes, dust to dust." Evadne's sister began to cry, and an uncle put his arm around her. There was a brief meeting of the Zoo Club at the reception afterward. They sang the club song. Lawyers, social workers, and teachers, all young girls again for one final moment.

She worked well into her eighties. She left a heritage of achievement and service. We do not control the hour or the manner of our death. But we have a say in what will remain of our lives after they are gone.

Tuesday in Lent IV

Wilt thou forgive those sins through which I run,
and do run still, though still I do deplore?
HYMN 141, JOHN DONNE (1573–1631)

Now, it's not that I don't know what to do. I know what to do. I read every fitness magazine as soon as it hits the newsstand. I think a lot about fiber and grams of fat, about my target heart rate, about my upper body workout. I have used—with great success—a method of combating cravings that has enabled me to pass by some pretty yummy treats without feeling deprived. I have expanded my list of appropriate indulgences—lovely fragrant bath, a phone call from a friend, a spin of a favorite record on the stereo—as substitutes for the food with which I have rewarded myself all my life. I have been very successful.

Why, then, do you suppose that I often just don't make use of the things I know? Why do I skip meals, when I know having done so will make me overeat later? Why do I stay in bed instead of going to the gym, telling myself something pious about being middle-aged and needing my sleep? Why do I get off on the wrong foot in the morning by having a breakfast I know signals overindulgence for the rest of the day? Why do I not keep a food diary, when I know it helps me? Why do I set myself up to fail?

Beats me. I just haven't a clue, and I've puzzled over the psychology of eating for a long, long time. I've come to the conclusion that it really doesn't matter *why* I do these things. What matters is *how* I'm going to do something else instead. What matters is whether I can find my way into the kind of behavior I want to have today, without worrying about whether or not I'm going to do so tomorrow or whether I did so yesterday.

Yes, God does forgive these sins. And my weakness against them. I'm not on my own against the stubbornness of my personal demons. None of us are alone with our demons. They may be stronger than we are, but God is stronger than they are.

Wednesday in Lent IV

The universe your glory shows.
HYMN 144, LATIN TRANSLATED BY ANNE K. LeCROY (B. 1930)

The Palestinian hills were dark at the time of Christ. They still are. Cities in those days didn't illuminate the night sky the way they do now, veiling the stars from our view in a competing pink or yellow glow. The stars stood out in the black night all over the world then, seeming to protrude from it, hanging in the heavens like fat, glowing fruit one might just reach up and pluck. Modern people have to journey far away from the city to see stars like that, but everyone could see them in those days.

You look up at the heavens, black sky studded with white fire, and you know your smallness. Of course God lives there, you think. Of course angels live there. You remember the psalm: What is a mortal, that God is mindful of him? You have heard of wizards and astrologers who can decipher the secrets of the stars, but you are no wizard. You are just a shepherd, or a shopkeeper, or a tentmaker, or a soldier like your father before you, and you are unlikely ever to be anything else.

That's what's remarkable: The great God of the heavens and the earth, of all possible worlds, has come to you and become like you. It is a paradox: everything that exists is not too great to come to you. The world matters to God. Your life matters. And everything is changed. You don't get rich. You don't become immortal. You're still not superman. But the mighty hand of the creator, who formed the majestic earth, formed you. And forms you still. So that you can become the human being you are intended to be.

Thursday in Lent IV

Now let us all with one accord,
in company with ages past...

HYMN 146, ATTRIBUTED TO GREGORY THE GREAT (540–604)

Morning and Evening prayer don't always pack them in at St. Clement's. Very often, the officiant recites the Office alone: "O God, make speed to save us." And answers himself: "O Lord, make haste to help us."

"Should I do the whole thing even if I'm the only one there?" a new officiant asks.

"Well, you never *are* the only one there," I tell him. Across from the officiant's desk hangs an icon of St. Clement, first bishop of Rome, who met his death at the wrong end of an anchor tossed into the Tiber. Next to Clement is one of Jonathan Daniels, a seminary student who was martyred in 1964 during the civil rights struggle in the South. Beside the officiant are two more icons, one of Christ and one of the Blessed Mother. "So you're never alone there," I finish, after having listed all the luminaries sharing space with us every morning and every evening.

These saints are not like stuffed animals or imaginary friends, although most church folk domesticate them in droll ways—we have a funny song we sing about St. Clement, set to the tune of "O My Darling Clementine." They are not mascots. They are not wishes. The are real. They lived in human history and continue to exist in the larger reality toward which all prayer reaches. They continue to be a part of us, and we of them, whether we feel their presence or not. I think the believer's faith in that truth is what makes it possible for us to be so familiar and irreverent about them. They are family.

And then there is your other family. The one you grew up with. The ones who have already died, leaving you behind here, a little more alone. The idea of the dead attending an eternal church service presents most of us with a picture of them as somewhat different than we remember. But consider this: What is church, after all, but a celebration of the love of God? Never mind that human versions of it often fall so far short of that ideal that people fall asleep in the middle of the service. It is supposed to be an experience of loving God and being loved back. It is supposed to be an experience of what we have named the communion of saints, the ongoing relationship between we who live here and they who live the larger life that contains ours.

So when you are alone with your prayer book and it says on the page, "The Lord be with you," don't feel foolish saying that greeting just because nobody is around. On the contrary: Everybody is around. Everybody who has ever lived, everybody you have ever loved or who has ever loved you, the people you knew and loved and the people you never knew—they live still, in the limitless love of God. "The Lord be with you," you tell them in your limited way, and they lovingly answer, "And also with you, dear one, and also with you."

Friday in Lent IV

For this, our foolish confidence,
our pride of knowledge and our sin,
we come to you in penitence;
in us the work of grace begin.
HYMN 148, DAVID W. HUGHES (1911–1967)

"Remember those tours?" I ask Trapper as we fill our wineglasses.

He rolls his eyes. "How could I forget? I can't believe we did that."

We used to pack all the actors and the music director and all the lights, programs, and sound effects into my van and take off for some church to which none of us had ever been to do a show in a space that none of us had ever seen. We would arrive about an hour before the curtain. Trapper would decide where to put the lights while I figured out how we were going to fit the show to the space. Then we would warm up a little, and go on at eight o'clock sharp. We did maybe eight or ten churches on a tour, and we did them all after having put in a full day at whatever our day jobs were. We'd roll back home at about midnight. And then we'd do it all again in a day or two.

I look back and wonder where I got the energy to do things like that. Where any of us got it. I drag myself off the train at the end of the day and barely say hello to Q before falling into bed. The old girl just ain't what she was.

I remember that younger woman very well. I remember that she really thought there was nothing she couldn't do. And she did accomplish a lot, and motivated others to accomplish much more than they ever thought they could. But I also remember that she felt superior to other people whom she believed to be too passive. That she shortchanged her family sometimes. It was pretty amazing. But it wasn't always very humble.

By the grace of God, people were touched and ennobled by our work. By the grace of God, we were too. By the grace of God, it didn't kill us. And by that same grace, I now know from where my power has always come: not from myself, but from God.

Saturday in Lent IV

Each heart is manifest to thee;
thou knowest our infirmity.

HYMN 152, ATTRIBUTED TO GREGORY THE GREAT (540–604)

"I don't know why I put up with this," the woman says, leaning back in her chair and closing her eyes. "Just when I'm about to murder her in cold blood, she comes in and does something so sweet I could cry. I've given up trying to figure her out."

I had a couple of those myself. Love is so elastic—it encompasses all manner of infuriating personality traits, stretching and stretching, but it never breaks. I know a woman whose son has been in and out of jail so many times we've both lost count, who has abused her trust so many times in so many ways that she can no longer allow him to know her address or her phone number. But she does not cease to love him. They keep in touch through me. I hold her number in a secret place, and patch him through when he appears. She continues to dream of a time when he will "get himself straightened out," as she puts it. I'm not sure just when that will be. Sometimes I think it will happen only in heaven.

God knows our frailties, our weaknesses, our inability to change things we wish with all our hearts were not as they are. There are many such things: harmful, hurtful parts of us so heavy that only God can lift them. Our inability is to be expected; we are human. So we do well to learn to call upon God in our weakness and to learn it early.

The Fifth Sunday of Lent

For righteousness and peace will show their faces
to those who feed the hungry in their need,
and wrongs redress, who build the old waste places,
and in the darkness shine.

HYMN 145, PERCY DEARMER (1867–1936)

It is not food pantry day, but a man is here asking for two bags. His wife and children are home, he says, and they have nothing to eat. We rummage in the back and produce the bags. As I hand them to him, I cannot help but notice that he has liquor on his breath. I invite him to services on Sunday and he says he will be there. I wonder if he will remember.

Might he sell the food instead of taking it home to his family? I'm sure I don't know, nor do I know how much a can of chicken parts is worth on the street. People often ask questions like that about the food pantry, questions that reveal the expectation that the poor may somehow get something to which they

83

are not entitled. Two bags of government surplus food, say, instead of one. Your spare quarter. The signs in the subway and in the train station admonish us not to give to people who ask for money. "They just use it to buy drugs," someone mutters when a panhandler asks me for money, and I don't know for sure that they don't.

How long would it take me to find a paper cup and stand on a street corner shaking it back and forth if I were hungry? Or, for that matter, if I were an addict and needed a fix, a need I know something about, having once been a cigarette smoker? How long would it take me to go to a church and ask the priest for money? It is hard to imagine myself doing any of these things, but there must have been a time when the man with liquor on his breath couldn't imagine going to a church for food.

I have a friend who was a crack addict. She is angered by talk that betokens suspicion of the poor, and it's certainly not because she thinks all poor people are honest and drugfree. "Addicts get hungry, too, you know," she says quietly when such a thing comes up in a group, and people remember just where she's been. None of us really know what is in another person's heart, or what is in his future. Usually we know only his present need.

Monday in Lent V

Wilt thou forgive that sin which I did shun
a year or two, but wallowed in a score?
   HYMN 141, JOHN DONNE (1573–1631)

I remember something frightening: Once I stopped smoking for about eight months and then started again *for no reason*. Somebody just offered me a cigarette and I took it. I smoked it with no ill effects and thought it no big deal. But my toe was in the door; within a week or two, I was a smoker again. And a heavier smoker than I had been before I quit.

It wasn't a moment of particular stress. I wasn't angry or particularly tired or anxious. There was absolutely no good reason for doing it, and yet I did it anyway. I still get scared just thinking about it. To this day, I don't like to think about the act of smoking. I am afraid that if I can visualize it, I will do it, and I think I'm right about that.

I remember the peculiar despair I felt about my habit, the tortured rationalizations I undertook to explain to myself why it was all right that I smoked. Why it was a matter of my civil rights. Why the fact that I was a good person in so many ways somehow made it okay to kill myself slowly and injure others in the process. I am still ashamed of the way my children hated my smoking, and of how little I cared.

It could indeed be said that I "wallowed" in that particular sin. Addicts *do*; their behavior isolates them from others, forces them into a smaller and smaller circle that eventually includes only other addicts. These days, cold as it is, the sidewalk in front of any office building is home to a clump of grim-faced people hunched over their cigarettes. They can't be inside with their colleagues. They have to stay outside with their cigarettes.

God certainly forgives our weakness. God longs for us to put down our burdens and come inside where it's warm. It is we who cannot believe that this is so. We think we have to do it all by ourselves, and we know we cannot. As so we stand outside, self-isolated. Until, at last, we are sick and tired of being sick and tired, as the saying goes. And then we knock. And the door to genuine self-love and sanity opens wide.

Tuesday in Lent V

Now nearer draws the day of days
when paradise shall bloom.

HYMN 144, LATIN TRANSLATED BY ANNE K. LeCROY (B. 1930)

Easter's on its way. Baskets of lurid plastic grass in a shade of green not found in nature nest staring chocolate rabbits and foil-wrapped eggs in the store window. The familiar boxes of egg dye wait in tantalizing stacks at the supermarket, which has laid in a store of smaller eggs especially for dying. The florist wants you to send faraway relatives a special Easter centerpiece, and in a corner of the gas station's parking lot, pots of white lilies and azaleas stand in rows, with palm crosses and sheaves of palm for the graves of your loved ones who have died.

All of these things are about the renewal of life, the upside of the mortal cycle of birth to life to death. They are all about coming to life again. The people who buy them may not know this—they adorn the graves because their mothers and fathers did it. Because it's what you do on Easter. But that's only because of what Easter *is*.

At the church's beginning, birth in Christ was often celebrated in the catacomb: the city's burial places. The first Christians were very close to death and understood it as the gate to rebirth. We die to the old life, they thought, and so it made a lot of sense to baptize in proximity to a tomb.

I've observed my Lenten fast. Most of the time it has made me more prayerful, although sometimes it has just made me more cranky. In observing the fast, I've died a little to this life, tasted just a bit of what it is to lose the world and its pleasures. Just a bit. I will one day taste it all. One day, paradise will bloom for me and I will see it as it is. I won't have to wonder about what lies beyond this life; I'll know.

Wednesday in Lent V

***Lord, who throughout these forty days for us didst fast and pray,
teach us with thee to mourn our sins, and close by thee to stay.***
HYMN 142, CLAUDIA FRANCES HERNAMAN (1838–1898)

Most of all, we don't want to be alone. We may long for some peace and quiet,
assaulted as we are by the needs of other people all day. But we don't want there
to be no one for whom we matter. We want somebody to be there.

People who are dying want that. They are embarked upon a fearsome journey, and it looks, at first glance, like a journey into oblivion. "I'm afraid to go
see him—what do I say?" someone says about a friend who is terminally ill,
and she stays away. But the dying one doesn't expect pearls of wisdom from
his visitors. Just your presence is enough—your brief presence, usually, since
people who are dying don't feel well and need to rest. Tell him you love him, if
you're built that way. Or don't—talk about baseball instead, if that's what

your friendship has been about. But you don't need to talk much on his account. He knows who you are.

As death comes nearer, something extraordinary happens. The dying one becomes more resident in the next world than in this one. Less tied to the existence he has known. This can be seen in a certain detachment from the people around him, a quietness with regard to interacting with them. Sometimes the family is hurt by this—doesn't he care that we're being separated? But this detachment is a blessing for the dying, a natural anesthetic against the pain of separation. It enables him to focus on the difficult task at hand: leaving this existence for another. It is like the quieting in the womb mothers usually note as childbirth becomes imminent. Both the baby and the dying person are gathering strength for the journey.

In life, in death, it is the same: Whenever we appear to be completely alone, Jesus is there. We began life with God, and we return to God when we die. When we can no longer reach out for the hand of the one we love, he grasps our hands firmly and helps us across.

Thursday in Lent V

Help us, lest in anxiety, we cause your Name to be betrayed.
HYMN 146, ATTRIBUTED TO GREGORY THE GREAT (540–604)

What we do not have is certainty. Is there a way I can know beyond doubt that my actions are in accordance with the will of God? Will I find respite from the uncertainties of modern life in the pages of Holy Scripture? Can I fully understand what the truth is and know beyond doubt that I am not in error? No. All I can do is try, knowing before I begin that my effort will be less than perfect. That I won't get it all just right. And being gentle enough on myself, and humble enough before others, to accept my limitations. I can never be absolutely sure. But I still must try to understand, because one of the things that makes me a human being is trying to understand.

This is not a particularly attractive idea, sounding as it does like a fair amount of work. No wonder the systems of belief that promise quick inerrancy flourish in the present anxious age: the magic crystals, the Peruvian mystical knowledge, the secret key that unlocks everything—and the magic Bible, the book that spells it all out for you in easy-to-digest little pellets that eliminate the discomfort of doubt. I can understand the lure of a life without uncertainty. I just don't think it's a very real life. No wonder fundamentalists often seem grim: It takes a lot of energy to assure themselves and others that there are no contradictions save "seeming" ones, that everything makes sense, that nothing happens without a reason, that we have a complete compendium of unambiguous recipes for every difficult decision in life. Most people over the age of twelve just don't experience life that way.

But if we're not looking at quick and easy recipes for certainty when we read the Bible, what are we doing? If we're on our own anyway, if the centuries that have intervened between the ancient writers and ourselves have so altered circumstances that we frequently cannot take their words at face value, why bother with them at all?

Because we have them. Because people long dead, whose names we will never know, thought they were important enough to copy out by hand, day after day and night after night, by candlelight or firelight in cold, drafty rooms. Because we are unable fully to understand about half of the world's literature if we are unfamiliar with them, since it presupposes familiarity with these texts.

But, most of all, because God speaks in them. Not always very clearly, and hardly ever simply. But the sacred writings to which we are heir are holy. The conversation about the soul and its journey in which we participate when we read them, a conversation that spans centuries and straddles cultures—this conversation is a crucible from which wisdom and goodness emerge. It may not be the same wisdom and goodness that emerged from it when it was first written down, or when it was read in the ninth century, or the nineteenth. But the conversation continues.

Friday in Lent V

To bow the head in sackcloth and in ashes,
or rend the soul, such grief is not Lent's goal;
but to be led to where God's glory flashes,
his beauty to come near.

HYMN 145, PERCY DEARMER (1867–1936)

Catch me in the wrong mood and this chirpy little Lenten hymn annoys me immensely. "God forbid anybody should ever be anything less than ecstatic every minute of every day," I am apt to mutter to myself. I am reminded of my generation's almost complete inability to take responsibility for its own errors: For the baby boomers, everything is someone else's fault. It seems to undo the soberness intrinsic to the project of taking stock of oneself, to insist on skating over the very real obstacles to the workings of God's grace that I have indeed been known to erect in my soul. There is such a thing as inappropriate shame

94

and guilt. But not all repentance is inappropriate. There are occasions when sackcloth and ashes are just the right attire.

But then, the words to this hymn were not written by a baby boomer. Percy Dearmer died in 1936. He lived through the first World War and the worst of the Great Depression, two events that shook the self-confidence of the entire world. This plea for hopefulness must be seen against the backdrop of a despair that was new in a world only just beginning to be conscious of itself as a world, as one place with one destiny.

People who can't identify the dark places in their own souls are better off if they learn to do so. But people who live in despair need to hear of hope. Need to hear of a divine glory that "flashes." And draws them powerfully and lovingly to itself, no matter how hopeless the world through which they journey may appear.

Saturday in Lent V

And through these days of penitence, and through thy Passiontide,
yea, evermore, in life and death, Jesus! with us abide.

HYMN 142, CLAUDIA FRANCES HERNAMAN (1838–1898)

The very first Christians focused less on penitence than on the preparation for the events leading up to Jesus' crucifixion and resurrection. In Western Christianity, penitence came to dominate Lenten observance as the centuries passed, so that the forty days were experienced primarily in terms of individual self-examination and repentance. The idea of the Atonement, the death of Jesus for our sins, almost completely eclipsed any other notion of what the sacrifice of the Son of God might mean.

But there are other notions. The Eastern Church always found the idea of God becoming human more interesting than the idea of human sinfulness. Heaven is very real for the Orthodox, and the scandal of heaven touching earth in Christ absorbs the mind of that part of the church much more than does the human drama itself. The reenactment of the events of Holy Week is theatrical and powerful in Greece, reminding us that theater has its origins in liturgy.

Back and forth we go: from our own drama to the great drama of incarnation and redemption, from me and my own limits to Jesus and his paradoxical ones. The God who chooses to be bounded by our boundaries, accepting in love what we endure out of necessity. The God who limits the unlimited divine self.

Often, I dream that I can fly. I stretch forth both my arms and leap, and I soar up over trees and housetops and telephone wires. In the dream, I see an obstacle before me and wonder if I can surmount it. Then I remember that I can fly and begin my confident ascent. The feeling is one of being limitless. When I awaken, that peaceful confidence lingers for a few moments. When I realize that it was only a dream, I am always a little disappointed.

Was the incarnation like that, only in reverse? Was Jesus aware of his power, power that he was not to use in overcoming the power of evil arrayed against him?

Did he move through his life among us holding it in check, move through those last terrible days and allow them to unfold for him as they would have unfolded for any common criminal? So we believe.

Palm Sunday

***To thee before thy passion they sang their hymns of praise;
to thee, now high exalted, our melody we raise.***

HYMN 154, THEODULPH OF ORLEANS (D. 821); TRANSLATED BY JOHN MASON NEALE (1818–1866)

The liturgy of Palm Sunday is one of our more theatrical ones: a procession, palm branches. Usually people read the story of Jesus' arrest and crucifixion as if it were a play. In some congregations, it *is* a play, with costumes and props, the whole nine yards. Theater is old in the church, as old as the Psalms, older. It's pretty clear that the worship of Jesus' day had for many years included singing and musical instruments and dance: Harps are mentioned, and drums, and timbrels—whatever that is—singers, everyone in his or her own way offering the best there was to the glory of God. Simply the best—every artist knows what that is. The feeling of having stretched as far as you can stretch. The happy exhaustion of having given it all. Knowing it was really, really good.

Clearly, there is a place in the life of faith for the arts, deployed with excellence in the service of the faith. They sprang from the church. It is time for the church to acknowledge and claim this fact as a theological and pastoral gift: not an extra little frill for those who happen to enjoy that sort of thing, but central to the human response to God.

Theological? Yes. When the human being stretches as far as possible, tests the limits of training and skill, she is fulfilling God's command: "Be fruitful and multiply." Did you think that was just about having babies? The world is filled and nurtured in all kinds of ways besides the obvious one of procreation. The writer. The singer. The actor. The metal worker. The painter. The dancer. The sculptor. God gives us gifts and we husband them carefully. We grow them in the garden of our lives. We adorn the church with them, in every medium the human mind and hands and body can invent. For the Christian, there is nothing that speaks of the human condition that does not also speak powerfully of God.

Pastoral? Absolutely. The arts ennoble both artist and patron. To create is to join in the work of the creator. The awkward teenager who becomes self-confidently alive in a walk-on role in a play. The rambunctious fourth-grader who discovers within himself the capacity for self-discipline in the choir, connecting with an ancient tradition of excellence and reverence that will remain with him as long as he lives. The middle-aged woman who rejoins her girlhood self in singing; the friends and relatives who see a side of her they never knew existed. The professional actor, cynical from his years in a tough profession, who feels for the first time a glimmer of faith from working in this sacred setting. Through the arts, the people of God come to know one another more fully, more as God knows each of us. They acquire the authoritative voice of interpreters of God's action in the world. They sing and dance and paint one small piece of the sacred story.

Monday in Holy Week

Who was the guilty? Who brought this upon thee?
Alas, my treason, Jesus, hath undone thee.
'Twas I, Lord Jesus, I it was denied thee:
I crucified thee.

HYMN 158, JOHANN HEERMANN (1585–1647); TRANSLATED BY ROBERT SEYMOUR BRIDGES
(1844–1930)

Because a concept is very central to Christian faith, does that mean that it must appear in every document that calls itself Christian, no matter what its purpose? Forgiveness, redemption through suffering, the identity with Christ through the cross: These are important Christian teachings. But sometimes they can be dangerous.

The church has often used Scripture to countenance oppression (the use of Philemon to baptize the American institution of chattel slavery being the most shameful example, although there are all too many others). It is possible to do this because the Hebrew and Christian Scriptures are layered through time and across ancient society, bringing many voices to bear on the experience of God. Much is made these days, in circles of folk who want to take Scripture seriously, of not "picking and choosing" congenial emphases in seeking to live a life informed by Scripture. The fact is, though, that we will all "pick and choose" among the many viewpoints in Scripture, and it is inevitable that we will do so. The Bible is very rich, as is the body of Christian teaching that has made use of it, and the whole of it cannot be stuffed into every discussion.

The idea of joining Christ in suffering is one of our teachings that has often been perverted to the ends of the powerful. Victims of domestic abuse have heard all about the redemptive power of their suffering and their duty to forgive many times, and they will hear all about it many times in the future. And yes, it is true that Jesus is close to us when we are in pain, and it is true that an inability to forgive will ultimately retard our own healing. I'm just not sure that victims of abuse need to hear it quite so much when they are still in the situation. Maybe they need to hear more about other equally scriptural Christian concepts: the stance of God on the side of the oppressed, the deliverance of the people of

Israel from Pharaoh. Most people think that forgiveness is something we must "come up with" in order to get right with God, when it is actually a gift from God, not something we come up with at all. Forgiveness does not mean that history has not occurred or that the abuse has somehow not happened, or that a psychological "Oh, what the heck, that's okay" state has somehow been achieved. Whatever it means in an individual case, it is certainly something that takes time. Premature emphasis on forgiveness will be difficult for someone accustomed to punishment to hear as anything but counsel to acquiesce in her own abuse. Insisting on forgiveness long before an emphasis on it is appropriate may prevent a well-meaning friend from doing what she really can do in God's name: empower, strengthen, comfort, and powerfully direct the abused person to focus on God's saving might and how it can show in her life.

Tuesday in Holy Week

Here in o'erwhelming final strife
the Lord of life hath victory,
and sin is slain, and death brings life,
and earth inherits heaven's key.

HYMN 163, CLEMENT OF ALEXANDRIA (170?–220?); PARAPHRASED BY
HOWARD CHANDLER ROBBINS (1876–1952)

It is a tough audience: Everyone in the room has lost a child, some more than one. My assignment is to speak to them on the topic "Where Was God When My Child Died?" We begin by listing all the inane things anyone has ever been told by a well-meaning comforter: that God needed another angel in heaven, so he took your little Tommy. That your five-year-old was removed to the safety of heaven, where she will never be tempted to sin. That God took your child to test you, or to punish you, or to punish your mom and dad because doesn't it say in the Bible that sins of the parents will be visited on the children? That God loves your child even more than you do, so he took her to be with him forever and ever, blah blah blah.

Person after person shouts out a platitude, and the assembly laughs grimly at each one. I write them all on the board. It feels good to lay them all out there. Then I talk a bit about how things just happen, for no reason, about how meaning comes from tragedy only after it has happened, not before. About how the unanswerable "Why?" doesn't bring healing, and how the more pragmatic "What?", as in "What can happen in light of what has happened?", is the only way to even begin mending a broken heart.

I know that I have offended some of the people in the group, who came to it hoping that I would provide a rational and satisfying answer to the "Where was God?" question. One man shakes his head in a silent no as I speak, and then states angrily that Jesus is Lord of all and that everything that happens is by his will. I apologize again for giving offense. I know that he is not ready for God to be anything other than the mighty king who always gets his way.

But God is a mystery. The gift of life is a mystery, and so is the fact of death. It comes to all of us, as it came to Jesus, much too soon. There appears to be little we can do beyond the dictates of common sense to determine when it will come. Sooner or later, we all enter the mystery: a reality far beyond this one, one of which we are only barely able to speak. But really, the only way to learn life in Christ is to live it. The life itself teaches us.

Wednesday in Holy Week

Sing, my tongue, the glorious battle;
of the mighty conflict sing;
tell the triumph of the victim,
to his cross thy tribute bring.
HYMN 166, VENANTIUS HONORIUS FORTUNATUS (540?–600?)

To say that we do gain strength from enduring pain is not at all the same thing as saying that this is what pain is for. We have an ignoble tradition with regard to Christian suffering: Although we are joined to Christ through all of our crosses, overemphasizing it here in Holy Week has often produced the masochistic glorying in suffering and eschewing of remedy that is Christian neurosis at its worst. You do get stronger from suffering, but it would be a perverse choice to volunteer for suffering in order that you might become strong, or to believe that in escaping abuse you are abandoning Christ on the cross.

So our liturgy offers a balance between pain and deliverance, despair and hope. It is no accident that the experience of the Israelites at the Red Sea is so important at this time of year. It is the central deliverance experience of Israel, and it formed the basis for the early Christian analysis of the significance of Jesus' life, death, and resurrection. It belongs in this week, which is, at bottom, one about deliverance by the mighty arm of God. It is no accident that the Eucharist remains up until Holy Saturday a steady presence in all the Holy Week liturgies. We are not allowed to forget our hope, even when we are face-to-face with human despair.

So the victim triumphs through the cross. Henceforth, all our trials are sanctified.

Maundy Thursday

Thirty years among us dwelling,
his appointed time fulfilled,
born for this, he meets his passion,
this the Savior freely willed.

HYMN 166, VENANTIUS HONORIUS FORTUNATUS (540?–600?)

Anna has it in her house now: a plain wooden coffee table her father made before she was born. Like so many things in our family, the table is not what it once was: It used to have hinged extensions on all four sides so you could lift the top off the legs and use the table as a tray. But a couple of the hinges broke, so we removed all the flaps. Now there are marks where the hinges uses to be, but no hinges.

And, of course, there's the bullet hole.

The kids and the baby-sitter were in an odd state of excitement when I walked in. "Look," my older daughter commanded, pulling me by the hand into the living room and pointing at the coffee table. I saw nothing untoward at first; everything looked pretty much as it should have. "No, look at the corner," she said, while the baby-sitter stood in the door and Anna lifted her arms and whimpered. I scooped her up and saw the bullet hole at the same time.

"She was standing right there where you are, and the bullet came down right beside her," said the baby-sitter, a little nervous. "Another inch and it would have gone right through her head." In the ceiling above the table was a jagged hole. I reached underneath the table to feel the exit hole. Splinters of wood came away in my hand. My mouth went dry.

"It was the boy upstairs. He was playing with his father's gun," the baby-sitter said. "Do you want to talk to him?"

I didn't want to talk to him. Not that red-hot minute. I wanted to look at my baby's eyelashes against the curve of her cheek. I buried my nose in her golden curls and thought of them matted with blood, thought of her little body in its corduroy overalls slumped motionless over the table, of shards of her skull on the carpet below. She began to wiggle impatiently and I set her down. She circled the table, inching her way around it, holding on with one hand. Just that week,

Anna was deciding whether or not to start walking on her own. She used the table as a security measure while she worked it all out. She was always standing by the table. Just another inch. A narrow escape. Anna's life was spared. We were spared her loss by an inch.

"Sing to the Lord, for he has triumphed gloriously," Miriam and her friends sang on the banks of the Red Sea. "The horse and its rider has he hurled into the sea." Their people had been spared, walked across the Red Sea on dry land: their brothers, their sisters and mothers and fathers, their children. Three thousand Egyptian soldiers had just died horribly right before their eyes, someone else's brothers and sons—mired in the mud, helpless against the tons of water that roared in on them and covered them forever. "Especially suitable for use during the Easter season" is the Prayer Book's helpful suggestion. I know some people who refuse to sing this one at all. "You want me to sing a song about how God killed off our enemies so we could be spared? I don't think so."

The deliverance of the children of Israel at the Red Sea, recounted in the Book of Exodus, was the signal salvation event of Israel's self-understanding: "We were almost destroyed, and then a miracle happened and we were saved." A miracle for Israel, maybe, but quite another thing for Egypt. To the children of Israel, God's hand in this deliverance was obvious. They simply did not think of the Egyptian widows and orphans made that day. Other times would come to them in the centuries that followed, hints of what else it might mean to be chosen by God. It would not always be a simple matter of being spared. Centuries later, things would get bad enough that Isaiah could describe God's choosing of Israel as the choice of a sacrificial victim: "But he was pierced for our transgressions, crushed for our iniquities; the chastisement he bore restored us to health, and by his wounds we are healed."

We seem to have a hard time holding onto this thought. We slip continually back to an earlier way of understanding God: God as the obedient genie who helps us out of all the really tight spots. We keep expecting this, even though life teaches us otherwise at so early an age: Do you know anyone over twelve who really thinks that God's love means nothing bad will ever happen? No. But why, then, do so many of us wonder about God's love when we lose someone dear, when we sicken and die ourselves, when we are not spared?

Jesus was God-among-us, Christians believe, walking the earth as we walk it: a life pointedly without the victories upon which we so often depend to certify

God's love as real. God-among-us as a loser, not as a winner. He does not hop nimbly down off the cross after his three hours of suffering and say, "See? Nothing to it!" *Au contraire.* Whatever you think about his identity or even about his existence, what we see in his story is a life ending in early, shameful death. Not even God escapes.

And yet, God stays. In life, in death, God abides. Another inch and there would be no Anna now, no one for her sister to chat with on the phone, no one for me to worry over and scold. The unthinkable would have been part of our family's history for years now. And God would abide in the horror of it. Abide in the sorrow, in the earth's unjust loss of yet another young life, lived in the love of God and lost in that love. And in that love would have been our healing.

Another inch. We did not have to walk that inch. We have had to walk others. I did not sing and dance our deliverance that day. I sat quietly and realized that we are fragile beings, that life is very brief. That the tiny child stillborn minutes ago and the old lady in France who is 120 years old and remembers Van Gogh live lives not substantially different in their brevity. An inch, more or less.

But they go on when they end. The death from which Jesus is raised reminds us: We are not delivered here. Being chosen doesn't mean that you always win. It doesn't make your inch any longer. The way to eternal life does not skirt death: It goes right through it.

But death does not defeat it. It can take our heart's blood and sprinkle it contemptuously in the dust, but God will raise us up. The iron door of death may slam shut, and we may hear it resound our whole lives long, but its permanence is only here. It is not a part of the reality that contains this one. What we see here is not all there is. To allow the spiritual life to be circumscribed by the test of personal material prosperity or physical well-being would be to deprive ourselves of something we're all going to need, sooner or later: a context of our lives that is larger than they are.

Good Friday

Were you there when they crucified my Lord?
Oh! Sometimes it causes me to tremble, tremble, tremble.
Were you there when they crucified my Lord?
HYMN 172, AFRICAN AMERICAN SPIRITUAL

This week: A young woman drops dead in the gym at school. Lovely. Funny. Twenty-one years old. "She was an angel," her boyfriend tells me, his voice dissolving into a sob. "An angel." He tells me he doesn't care about anything now, and doesn't think that he ever will again.

Also this week: A young priest dies of AIDS. Gifted. Funny. Humane. "They won't let me in," he whispers, as the end approaches. He begs to be taken back to his church. "I know they'll let me in there."

Also this week: A young soldier walks a few paces off the road near a Bosnian village and steps on a land mine. He is dead before he reaches the hospital.

Identity withheld pending notification of next of kin. The first American casualty. Probably not the last.

The mothers and fathers, the grandparents—they are still absurdly alive. Bargaining fruitlessly on the plane ride to pick up the body, in the taxi from the airport, frantically negotiating an exchange that cannot occur: their lives for the lives of their children. *If only it were me. Let this not have happened. Can it not please, please be me instead? Let us rewind this terrible film and begin again. Cover me with deadly sores, explode my flesh and my bones, shock my heart into useless spasms. Anything—but leave my child to grow old in my place. Do not doom me to life here on earth without my child.*

There is only silence.

The veil in the temple was rent in two. The sun was hidden behind a cloud, and the earth was in darkness for three hours. The world shook and rocks were split. Graves opened, and the dead were seen walking in the city streets. My world shuddered to an end and lay still.

Holy Saturday

Thy beauty, long desired, hath vanished from our sight;
thy power is all expired, and quenched the light of light.
Ah me! for whom thou diest, hide not so far thy grace:
show me, O Love most highest, the brightness of thy face.

HYMN 168, PAUL GERHARDT (1607–1676); TRANSLATED BY ROBERT SEYMOUR BRIDGES (1844–1930)

"At the cross, her vigil keeping." Not in your virginity, Mother of Christ, not in your purity, but in your suffering we know you best. There are those among us who behold your face in our mirrors each day. Men and women alike have seen themselves in you, have reached out their arms as you did to receive the lifeless bodies of their children in a final embrace. Those bodies whose swiftness and strength was their joy, whose preservation was their sacred trust, thrown contemptuously back in their faces by unconcerned Death. Nothing further can be done to you now. Everything has already been taken.

And afterward. The bleak afterward that threatens to last forever. After the funeral, after the flowers wilt, after the kind casseroles and special cakes have been discarded half-eaten. After all the socks and underwear have been given away. After the dog has ceased his mournful whimpers in the corner of the room. After all the photographs have been searched out and enlarged, all the casual notes and shopping lists in that familiar hand pressed in a book. After people have stopped asking how you're doing. After everyone else has gotten back to normal. After you have forgotten what normal was.

In your empty house, Holy Mary, in the small hours, you go from room to room. It is as if you are looking for something. Now you cannot see his life except through the lens of his death. Now every remembered joy seems to have antici-pated this sorrow. Now it seems that he knew what was ahead. Now it seems that he always knew, even when he was little. How could *you* not have known? There are even fleeting moments when you wish you had never known the joy of him. If you had never known the joy, you could not now know the anguish of it ripped from you. You remember your girlhood, a thousand years ago. You wish your mother and father were still alive.

His stunned friends visit you awkwardly. They do not know what to say to you. You steal glances at their broad shoulders, their muscled legs and arms, the energy that abounds in them even in shock and sorrow. You take their hands in yours and try not to think of his hands.

You know that you will keep on. Of course. There is no question of anything else. You know that people are concerned about you. People could not have been kinder.

At the edge of town, there is a tomb that holds the body you once held safe within your body. With friends who also remember him, you start down the dusty path toward it.

Easter Day

Arise, arise, arise! and make a paradise!
HYMN 145, PERCY DEARMER (1867–1936)

Bill and I were walking back to my place after dinner at Fedora, which is Bill's favorite restaurant. A bicycle passed us swiftly, its rider high on the seat and low over the handlebars, wearing a helmet and those black spandex shorts that people on bicycles wear today. "I really miss riding a bike," Bill said, and I nodded and said, "Yeah, I'll bet you do," as we turned up Eleventh Street and continued our slow walk. We always walk slowly, Bill and I, slower than I walk when I'm alone, because Bill's right side is paralyzed. He wears a heavy brace on his leg, and he holds one arm bent against his chest so his two arms don't swing like other people's do to help them along when they walk. Bill lurches from side to side when he walks—or, at least he did when he walked—but he can maintain a pretty decent clip when he gets going. Or rather, he used to.

I'm having a little trouble with my verb tenses right now where Bill is concerned. He's lying in a hospital bed now, blood seeping into his brain from a tumor buried somewhere deep within it. His walking days are over. His talking days, too, and the writing days that took their place (a little magic slate like we had when were kids: Bill's communications link to the world after his speech went last week). His seeing days are behind him. At thirty-five, the powers of his body are abandoning him, one by one, and his death is now very near. "I gave him the last rites yesterday," my colleague tells me on the phone. "I think he understood. I think he was making the responses, trying to make them, anyway: I mean, all he could do was groan."

We have lots of thirty-five-year-olds dying in New York—more than I ever thought I'd see, back in the days before I knew that the remaining decades of my ministry would be filled with young people dying. But Bill isn't dying of AIDS, as are all those others. He got this brain tumor when he was fourteen—almost died then, but they pulled him through, with only the paralysis to show for a terrible year's ordeal. "That must have been tough," I said when he was telling me about it one day at the coffee shop, and he smiled. "Yeah, you see, I had just realized I was gay," he said, "and when I got sick I thought God was punishing me." I stirred my coffee and said nothing; he talked about his Catholic upbringing and his guilt, about his self-loathing, about his terror and his pain. We talked, as we always do, about his recovery from the alcoholism and drug abuse in which he had buried that pain for a dozen years or so. We talk about what serenity means. What responsibility means. Bill's always beating himself up about his failures. I think about him struggling out of bed in the morning and strapping on his leg brace to go to work, and I tell him that he sure doesn't look like a failure to me.

We talk a lot about healing. We did, I mean, when Bill could talk. Eight years of sobriety is a powerful healing. Discovering a Christian faith that isn't all about shame and guilt is another; Bill's has come to know that the Higher Power that delivered him from the bondage of addiction is Jesus Christ. I would see him at the Eucharist, or at Morning Prayer, bowing from the waist in a solemn bow at the name of Jesus, and crossing himself very slowly and deliberately. He wears a cross around his neck—sometimes two or three crosses, and sometimes he wears a cross earring on one ear as well: Bill's quite a unique dresser. "I know that God doesn't hate me. I keep slipping into my old self-hatred," he says, "but I know that God doesn't hate me. It wasn't true that he made me sick because I was gay. That wasn't true."

"No, it wasn't," I tell him, and I feel myself shaking: I am so angry at whoever taught a young boy to believe in a God who would send him a brain tumor for being gay that I just don't trust myself to speak further. We talk about the love of God in guiding him toward sobriety and new relationships with people in AA, about the place of confession in his new life in Christ, about the presence of Christ in the body and the blood. "I stay away from the blood myself," he says, "a little too close to home. So is it really true that the bread alone is enough?" I tell him yes, it is really true. Bill loves to talk about the ins and outs of church tradition. Loves trick questions. He loves to visit the monastery. He attends the inquirers' class. Last year he was received into the Episcopal Church at the cathedral. "I don't know if my parents will come," he says wistfully. But they did come.

"Things are about the same," says his mother now when I call the hospital. "He's not really awake at all now. They say it won't be too much longer."

The body that now lies dying knows very well what it is to live with pain and weakness. But still his faith has made him well. He groans out the responses in the church's last anointing of his body on this side of heaven, inarticulate groans that mean "And also with you" and "Amen," as he prepares to leave his maimed physical body for his perfect spiritual one. His soul has gotten strong. His soul is what will remain. And his soul belongs to Christ, and he knows it. And it is enough. So Bill was healed—of so many things. That fourteen-year-old boy never rode a bike again. I think of him, the way he will be soon, and I send him this vision: In glory, Bill—strong, both arms free and both legs pumping hard, riding a bike as fast as the wind right into the city of God.